Birthdays, Numbers & More

Patty Blank

Outskirts Press, Inc.
Denver, Colorado

Outskirts Press
http://www.outskirtspress.com

ISBN: 1-59800-260-0
ISBN 13: 978-1-59800-260-7

Printed in the United States of America

Birthdays, Numbers & More

This small book will make a huge difference in your life. It was written with the intent to make everyone's life happier and easier by providing a little insight to the understanding of why people do the things they do. Hopefully this workbook will become worn and tattered because you will use it daily due to its value. The first section is a simple monthly calendar. Here is where you will keep a written record of the birthdays of all family members, friends, lovers and business partners. Basically, everyone you know. You will need the complete date; month, day and year of birth. With this basic information you will be able to use the second section of the workbook to get to know these people from the inside out. Everyone's birthday holds valuable information to who they truly are. And then the final section will give you a little more explanation of the whole picture by comparing the numbers. Before you write anything in this booklet, first figure out your own Lifepath number and read my description of whom you are. If you agree with what I have written pick up a pen and get started. Discover a quick and simple way to answer that life long question, "Why do people do the things they do?"

Birthdays

Birthdays have always been very special days for me all of my life. I grew up in a family that celebrated birthdays in a traditional way. My parents made us "kings" or "queens" for the day. We received more gifts than we ever did at Christmas. My mother made us our favorite meal. We had parties and all of our friends and relatives were invited. I remember my grandmother celebrating her birth month. As I got older and I moved away from my hometown I kept in touch with old friends by always remembering their birthdays and send cards and letters to them on their special day. I still do. All my grandparents and both parents have passed on. Once someone asked me how long it had been since my parents passed over. I could not remember. I have never paid much attention to the end of anything, but I always remember the beginning.

Please use this section of the workbook to keep a record of the birthdates of the people that mean the most to you. Check it regularly. These special people deserve to be treated as "kings" and "queens" on their special day. Buy them gifts, send cards, email them a special greeting. It will make you feel good inside to do this. Just imagine how it will make them feel.

January Birthdays

1____
2____
3____
4____
5____
6____
7____
8____
9____
10_______________________________________
11_______________________________________
12_______________________________________
13_______________________________________
14_______________________________________
15_______________________________________
16_______________________________________
17_______________________________________
18_______________________________________
19_______________________________________
20_______________________________________
21_______________________________________
22_______________________________________
23_______________________________________
24_______________________________________
25_______________________________________
26_______________________________________
27_______________________________________
28_______________________________________
29_______________________________________
30_______________________________________
31_______________________________________

February Birthdays

1____________________
2____________________
3____________________
4____________________
5____________________
6____________________
7____________________
8____________________
9____________________
10____________________
11____________________
12____________________
13____________________
14____________________
15____________________
16____________________
17____________________
18____________________
19____________________
20____________________
21____________________
22____________________
23____________________
24____________________
25____________________
26____________________
27____________________
28____________________
29____________________

March Birthdays

1 ____________________
2 ____________________
3 ____________________
4 ____________________
5 ____________________
6 ____________________
7 ____________________
8 ____________________
9 ____________________
10 ____________________
11 ____________________
12 ____________________
13 ____________________
14 ____________________
15 ____________________
16 ____________________
17 ____________________
18 ____________________
19 ____________________
20 ____________________
21 ____________________
22 ____________________
23 ____________________
24 ____________________
25 ____________________
26 ____________________
27 ____________________
28 ____________________
29 ____________________
30 ____________________
31 ____________________

April Birthdays

1___
2___
3___
4___
5___
6___
7___
8___
9___
10___
11___
12___
13___
14___
15___
16___
17___
18___
19___
20___
21___
22___
23___
24___
25___
26___
27___
28___
29___
30___

May Birthdays

1____________________
2____________________
3____________________
4____________________
5____________________
6____________________
7____________________
8____________________
9____________________
10____________________
11____________________
12____________________
13____________________
14____________________
15____________________
16____________________
17____________________
18____________________
19____________________
20____________________
21____________________
22____________________
23____________________
24____________________
25____________________
26____________________
27____________________
28____________________
29____________________
30____________________
31____________________

June Birthdays

1____
2____
3____
4____
5____
6____
7____
8____
9____
10____
11____
12____
13____
14____
15____
16____
17____
18____
19____
20____
21____
22____
23____
24____
25____
26____
27____
28____
29____
30____

July Birthdays

1 ____________________
2 ____________________
3 ____________________
4 ____________________
5 ____________________
6 ____________________
7 ____________________
8 ____________________
9 ____________________
10 ____________________
11 ____________________
12 ____________________
13 ____________________
14 ____________________
15 ____________________
16 ____________________
17 ____________________
18 ____________________
19 ____________________
20 ____________________
21 ____________________
22 ____________________
23 ____________________
24 ____________________
25 ____________________
26 ____________________
27 ____________________
28 ____________________
29 ____________________
30 ____________________
31 ____________________

August Birthdays

1____
2____
3____
4____
5____
6____
7____
8____
9____
10_______________________________________
11_______________________________________
12_______________________________________
13_______________________________________
14_______________________________________
15_______________________________________
16_______________________________________
17_______________________________________
18_______________________________________
19_______________________________________
20_______________________________________
21_______________________________________
22_______________________________________
23_______________________________________
24_______________________________________
25_______________________________________
26_______________________________________
27_______________________________________
28_______________________________________
29_______________________________________
30_______________________________________
31_______________________________________

September Birthdays

1____
2____
3____
4____
5____
6____
7____
8____
9____
10____
11____
12____
13____
14____
15____
16____
17____
18____
19____
20____
21____
22____
23____
24____
25____
26____
27____
28____
29____
30____

October Birthdays

1
2
3
4
5
6
7
8
9
10
11
12
13
14
15
16
17
18
19
20
21
22
23
24
25
26
27
28
29
30
31

November Birthdays

1 ______________________________
2 ______________________________
3 ______________________________
4 ______________________________
5 ______________________________
6 ______________________________
7 ______________________________
8 ______________________________
9 ______________________________
10 ______________________________
11 ______________________________
12 ______________________________
13 ______________________________
14 ______________________________
15 ______________________________
16 ______________________________
17 ______________________________
18 ______________________________
19 ______________________________
20 ______________________________
21 ______________________________
22 ______________________________
23 ______________________________
24 ______________________________
25 ______________________________
26 ______________________________
27 ______________________________
28 ______________________________
29 ______________________________
30 ______________________________

December Birthdays

1___
2___
3___
4___
5___
6___
7___
8___
9___
10___
11___
12___
13___
14___
15___
16___
17___
18___
19___
20___
21___
22___
23___
24___
25___
26___
27___
28___
29___
30___
31___

Numbers

Numerology is the study of life as seen in the numbers. Just as astrology is the study of life as seen in the stars. If you were to read an individual's numerological report and also their astrological chart, it would be like reading the same novel with different covers. The similarities of the results are amazing and prove to add strength to your faith and well-being.

This section of the workbook is designed to keep a record of your acquaintances' Lifepath numbers. This number of a person's chart is like a fingerprint. It is derived from the numbers of a person's birth date and no one can change those numbers. In this workbook the Lifepath number is the only calculation I will use to uncover the strongest vibration that appears in an individual's chart. It is a person's birth force. Its expression is the backbone of their existence. This number describes general characteristics, trends, talents and tendencies of those you would like to understand a little better.

To calculate one's Lifepath number simply add together all the numbers involved in their date of birth. Continue to add the double digits until a single digit is achieved. Example: 3-11-1971 3+1+1+1+9+7+1= 23 2+3=5

Now go back through the "Birthdays" section and calculate the Lifepath numbers of those who are near and dear to your heart and list them in the section of the workbook that describes that birth force number. When you have several names listed under a single Lifepath number you will begin to understand that number's vibration. It will then aid you in understanding that as individuals we have certain vibrations from the day of birth that will never ever change. Once you realize this you will accept everyone for who they are and realize no one can be changed. You cannot change your fingerprint and you cannot change yourself, or anyone else for that matter.

Lifepath 1

I am Me

Ambitious, strong-willed, determined and well organized, the number ONE'S aim is to express one's self. Understanding fully who they are makes them truly independent, with a mind of their own.

You can understand the different numbers simply by their symbol. Numerical symbols have been used for over 7000 years. Imagine, if you will, the first Homo sapiens, whether it be Adam and Eve or Neanderthal men, trying to communicate for the very first time. The strongest would take their finger and draw a straight, bold vertical line in the dirt, pound their chest and say ME.

ONES enjoy sports and athletics, be it solo events like tennis, boxing, skiing and auto racing or team events where they excess as the home run hitter, star quarterback or team captain. ONES use their mental capacity, along with control of self and any situation for the perfect strategy, pride in their abilities and the spirit to perform at the highest level. They like to win. Hence, they can become sore losers.

Keen intuition offers ONES a strong faith in self. So they rarely seek guidance or advice of others. This strong gut feeling also gives ONES a pioneer spirit, offering creativity and the opportunity to express their unique individuality.

Other characteristics:

- Dry sense of humor, can cut to the quick.
- Leaves the past behind, looks ahead with new ideas and a fresh start.
- Buys for quality, not for price.
- Impatient of rules and regulations, dislikes limitations or being told what to do.
- Dislikes carelessness and vulgarity, swearing is improper use of the English language.
- Has a very good memory.
- Not emotionally romantic.
- Not too materialistic, but has the ability to always get what they want.
- Selective of companions, seeks common interests, strengths and an equal to or higher IQ and talents.
- A day person, likes being in the light.

Challenges are sought and a strong drive for achievement is always apparent in a ONE. Efficiency is a must and executive abilities are inbred. ONES have all the attributes of an entrepreneur. They may also seek creative careers in writing or designing. Judgment careers also have their appeal, could be a lawyer or a doctor. ONES have such strong leadership qualities, an officer in the armed forces could fit, and maybe even Commander in Chief could be in the offering.

It is very possible during the formative years, the ONE person had to fight for their independence. They may have been born into a family with a domineering parent or maybe they were in constant conflict with a challenging sibling or childhood friend. Later they may have had to battle for authority with a teacher. If this Lifepath is a difficult one for the soul, it just may be the ONE has had a combination of many "independence" struggles. Regardless, at some point the ONE had to become self-centered, arrogant, stubborn and demanding of oneself. With statements like, "We will do it my way", " I'm first", " I know I am right" and " I never said that" they set out to prove their independence to the world.

The next step to this lesson for the ONE is using what they have learned for the good of all. The answer lies in the vibration of the numbers on either side. After ONE comes TWO, the peacemaker. ONES need to realize there is another side, another opinion besides their own, another way to find an answer. ONES need to learn to compromise and cooperate without losing their identity. ONES can stay in the driver's seat, they just need to realize they have passengers. And since the universe is a circle, NINE would be the vibration on the other side. ONES need to develop compassion and try to work on manifesting charisma, patience and balance. With these trades, the ONE can stop fighting to be the leader, they just "will" be the leader. As an adult, the ONE that truly has gained their independence has learned to accept criticism. They become generous with emotions and have learned to pass on their spirit. ONES will encourage the other dependent people of the world with statements like " Go for it", "Never say never", "You can do it", and "Nothing is impossible". A mature ONE will have learned to be diplomatic and to restrain their forcefulness.

This being the first of the numerological commandments is, in my opinion, the most important. ONE is so basic. Wake up every morning with the desire to do the best that you can, with the right attitude and also take time to help others in your path. If you can master this, the rest is a piece of cake. By expressing ONES self in a positive, generous, peaceful and sensitive way, the ONE will retain leadership and friendships forever.

Lifepath 1 Friends

Famous Lifepath 1 People

Walt Disney
Henry Ford
Billy Graham
Sammy Davis, Jr.
Dan Rather
Susan B. Anthony
Truman Capote
George Washington
Florence Nightingale
Ernest Hemingway
Mother Teresa
Walt Whitman
Calvin Klein
George Lucas
Napoleon
George Carlin
Ayn Rand
Sting
Steve Forbes
Martin Luther King, Jr.
Tom Hanks
Jacques Cousteau
George Clooney
Humphrey Bogart
Magic Johnson
Larry King
Colin Powell

Lifepath 2
I am Balanced

Supportive, understanding, impartial, friendly and tactful; this diplomatic peacemaker thinks of others' well-being and happiness before their own every time they are challenged. A TWO's aim in life is to establish and maintain harmony in this world. They are here to balance the scales of justice.

Back to the beginning of time and the drawing of our expressions in the sand, after the first man (Adam) declares himself as a straight bold line, the second person (Eve) is quick to draw two straight lines next to each other. But in haste they appear to be connected. The TWO wants everyone to know that it takes TWO to survive, to grow, to multiply.

The TWO represents opposites and pairs. There are many opposites in the world, i.e. black/white, left/right, male/female and many opposite points of view. The TWO's challenge is to gather all the facts and offer a compromise so a middle ground is prevalent and the opposites become pairs. Think of yin and yang, both are equal color and size, yet held together in the all-encompassing circle of the divine power. This is all done in a persuasive manner, never forceful. The TWO rarely dominates a situation, but prefers to remain the power behind the throne. They represent the stereotypical "woman behind her man".

During peaceful times, the TWO becomes the co-pilot or the loyal "Gal Friday". They support the person in charge, while remaining in the background. Others have the bright ideas and the TWO carries them out. Sometimes TWOS do all the work, while some other Lifepath gets all the glory.

TWOS have an innate sense of rhythm and timing. It only makes sense that someone so gifted in creating harmony would have natural grace and musical instincts. Imagine, if you will, the mother swaying with her child in her arms gently patting the back and singing a lullaby.

Everyone thinks they have good taste. Well, a TWO does. With their ability to see all, which is really seeing both sides as one, they know what is good.

Other characteristics:

- Happiest when married or at least involved in a cause.
- Very intuitive.
- Often seen as an apple polisher or a brown nosier.
- A good mixer, matchmaker, host or hostess.
- Pays great attention to detail.
- Careful with money, views it as security and hence will never overspend.
- Perfectionist, very determined about little things.
- Whole life is spent playing "follow the leader".
- Finds physical faults in self; feet too big, ears stand out, nose has a bump, too tall or too short.
- Fearful of standing alone in the world.
- Dislikes conflicts, but loves to kiss and make up.
- Likes pets, having one means never having to be alone.
- Has a delicate ego.
- Loves dawn and dusk, able to see both light and dark from one point.

Meditating, social work, religion and psychology are all professions that allow the TWO to interact with people on a one-to-one basis, while bringing harmony and peace. A career in banking, finance, or the stock market would allow the TWO control of the money for the good of many. Nursing, editing, lab assistant and secretarial work permits a TWO to be supportive. Accountants, librarians, actuaries, astronomers and statisticians are usually TWOS. These careers gather facts and put them where they belong. TWOS are the bearers of the light from within. TWOS may become mediums, psychics, numerologists or healers. A TWO prefers to stay out of the limelight, so more often than not, they choose not to become a dancer, musician or poet. However, it would be a good tool for relaxation, for it would give the TWO an outlet for their individuality.

The TWO is an angel child, eager to please even at a young age. They are easy to toilet train, readily give up the bottle, needs little discipline and rarely demand either parent's attention. The TWO is truly a peacemaker from birth. This may be the reason why parents seldom encourage or compliment the TWO child. They just do not feel there is a need to do so. If this is meant to be a difficult Lifepath lesson, the TWO may have been born into a family where one or both of the parents forbids, criticizes, chastises and ridicules the young TWO. Since TWOS respect their parents, these actions grant them an even stronger desire to obtain quiet beauty.

Often a TWO will be indecisive. They do not want to make a mistake or worse yet, bring attention to themselves. On an off day, the TWO is apathetic, disagreeable, nit-picky, fastidious, petty, sly, inconsiderate, deceptive, disinterested and down right rude. A TWO tends to tell a person what they think they want to hear, for they fear hurting other people's feelings with the truth. TWOS may appear to be a busybody, standoffish or supersensitive.

If a TWO can learn to find their own mental strength in their individuality and to be more positive while remaining true to themselves from the vibration of the ONE, and they can add the emotional joy of attaining harmony and beauty from the THREE, they will bring continuity, comfort, warmth and affirmation to all the world. This success will create the demand for the TWO's peacemaker skills and knowledge, and fulfill their underlying desire to be needed.

As the second of the numerological commandments, peace is a strong lesson to learn and enforce. It is important for all Lifepaths to see both sides of an issue. Everyone needs to be still and become balanced.

Lifepath 2 Friends

Famous Lifepath 2 People

Amelia Earhart
E.E. Cummings
Madonna
Rush Limbaugh
Michael Jordan
Dolley Madison
Joe Montana
Beatrix Potter
Diana Ross

Bobby Fischer
George Armstrong Custer
Kobe Bryant
Rosa Parks
Jack Kerouac
Norman Mailer
Mozart
Prince Charles
Dr. Seuss

John Glenn, Jr
Jennifer Aniston
Paris Hilton
Gwyneth Paltrow
Henry Kissinger
John McCain
George C. Scott
Ronald Reagan
Paul Simon

Lifepath 3
I am Happy

Witty, spirited and sparkling this happy-go-lucky optimist inspires others to expand and grow while putting great big smiles on their faces. This radiant joy giver vibrates to creative self-expression through words, music and art. The THREE is a performer, an animated comic ready to share a joke at any given time.

The horizontal straight lines show a passive nature. The curves or slants of any written number represent love and joy. THREES are either a combination of the two or all love and joy, depending on how you write the number THREE. The straight vertical lines of a written number represent independence and strength. You cannot write a three with vertical lines.

THREE is an emotional number that provides the bearer with an open heart wanting true happiness for all of their friends, of which they have many. Companionships are valued. Gregarious, merry, considerate and cordial, they may encounter many loving, romantic relationships. THREES communicate easily, being able to tap into deep emotional feelings they find important to express. THREES love pleasure and spontaneity. They are very accepting and tend not to worry much about anything. THREES go with the flow.

THREE is a charm. What comes in threes? Body/mind/soul, father/mother/child, past/present/future. Give a little thought to the third item of each of these trinities and you will have a better understanding of the path of a THREE. An interesting fact to note: the blending of the three primary colors produces the colors of the rainbow. I would declare that to be creative and joyful.

How many times have you chuckled at the naïve and uncomplicated view of life as seen through the eyes of a child? The THREE is that child. Life is simple for the THREE. It may appear that THREES never attract misfortunes. The truth is, due to their innate optimism and ability to maintain an open heart and mind, problems are solved easily, never becoming desperate, anxious or depressing. THREES tend to keep a molehill, a molehill.

Enthusiastic, eager and clever, THREES make dreams come true. Having an innate talent for visualization keeps them on the lighter side of life. THREES are quick learners, acquiring insight and knowledge without effort. They also find it easy to memorize.

Other characteristics:

- Strong need to belong, it is vital to a THREE.
- Very convincing, able to make others see what possibilities exist.
- Maintains a sunny disposition.
- Bypasses the practical.
- Impatient with slow thinkers.
- Usually generous with possessions as a token of shared love.
- Tends to talk with their hands.
- Loves the easy life.
- Dresses fashionably, always in style, aware of what is new.
- Talks too much, sometimes at the wrong time.
- Vulnerable to criticism, doesn't want the bubble to burst.
- Tends to rationalize behavior.
- May be frivolous.
- A gift giver, usually adult toys.
- Romantic flirt, loves dating.
- Likes the day as well as the night, at their best all the time.

THREES are intellectual with a high command of the English language. They may choose journalism as a livelihood, or teaching and lecturing. With a true appreciation of the beauty in the world, they may decide to use painting, sculpting, singing or dancing as a way of expressing their creative imagination. THREES artistic ability and humor may combine to produce an exceptional cartoonist or circus clown. With their exceptional gift of gab, they may become the born salesman.

As a child it was very important for the THREE's creativity to be recognized, to obtain a sense of acceptance. Praise for completed work would have boosted their desire to get things done. Firm disciplining would encourage understanding the rules. THREES develop a vivid imagination early, may tell tall tales or have make-believe friends. They always have great energy requiring mental stimulation and diversity.

THREE's lesson starts out easy enough, but at some point they realize life is not all play and no work. They have a tendency to scatter forces and become a jack-of-all-trades. They may put things off, procrastinating too long. Everyone has had bad days; on their bad days, the THREES lose their sense of humor and will become boastful, cocky, opinionated, irresponsible, superficial, envious, withdrawn, touchy and pompous. THREES need to ask themselves who they are creating for, their own enjoyment or that of others.

To conquer this lesson the THREE must look to the numbers before and after the THREE. They must learn receptivity and compromise from the TWO. True happiness is found when emotional experiences are shared. However, the major lesson is in knowing and understanding limitations. The FOUR will provide all this for the THREE. Build a foundation without losing the talent to visualize. If a THREE can become an adult without losing the child within, success is inevitable.

Joy is vital for existence. Joy to the World, the Lord has come! May we all see the lighter side to life?

Lifepath 3 Friends

Famous Lifepath 3 People

Andre Agassi
Jimmy Buffett
Alfred Hitchcock
Leonardo DaVinci
Anne Frank
John Travoltra
K.D. Lang
Imelda Marcos
Carlos Santana

Jane Austen
Fidel Castro
Charles Dickens
Julius Erving
John Wayne
Andrew Jackson
Evel Knievel
John Malkovich
Jennifer Lopez

David Bowie
Salvador Dali
Bill Cosby
F. Scott Fritzgerald
Hugh Hefner
Frida Kahlo
Ann Landers
Robert Duvall
Peter Jennings

Lifepath 4
I am Organized

Devoted, cool-headed, dependable, sensible, practical and trustworthy, this diligent bricklayer will build a strong foundation and then invite family and friends to stand up on it and feel secure and protected.

The FOUR is a reliable, dedicated worker; they go at their own pace, gathering all the facts and researching the details in order to get the job done right the first time. They hate to admit to mistakes, although they do learn from them. FOURS can come into a chaotic situation, take the time to access what is required to establish system and order, and with patience and perseverance will get the job done, always on time, if not a little early.

FOURS are solid, law-abiding, scrupulous citizens. They have a well-defined sense of values, conduct and morals that they live by. FOURS expect respect and dignity from others for their ability to perform a noble and creative job. They have their own version of what is right and wrong, along with strong likes and dislikes. FOURS can be stubborn, unbending and a bit rigid in their thinking.

Very frugal and thrifty, FOURS will always get their money's worth. They save money for emergencies. They pay their bills on time. FOURS like to be debt free. FOURS will often stash a twenty dollar bill in the back of the wallet or in a safe hiding place – just in case. FOURS dislike buying on credit, if they cannot afford it out right, they really do not want it. If they use their American Express Card it is for convenience sake and will be paid in full with each statement. They don't gamble or take chances, but FOURS investigate the situation completely and only go for the sure bets.

FOUR is the number of the earth. There are four seasons, four points on a compass and four elements (earth, wind, fire, water). Moses brought down the foundation on which to build a life on four stone tablets. A building block, a two-by-four, a safe deposit box and a square all have four sides. Can you see how the FOUR developed their characteristics?

The FOUR is a faithful, quiet, traditional, sincere and a loyal mate and partner. They are consistent and straight forward, a good provider. FOURS have a few close friends rather than loads of acquaintances. Probably because they would rather work than socialize. A true giver that sincerely shares everything and believes others should not go without if they have enough to go around. FOURS demonstrate emotion. Love is a feeling, an action of the heart. Anger, fear and jealousy are all emotions or reactions resulting from a threat of physical or mental harm.

A great problem solver, the FOUR does not act, think or perform with speed. Very methodical and careful, this person will base all efforts on sound practical reasoning. Conscientiously the FOUR will build a solid foundation properly or they risk its collapse having to start all over again from scratch.

Other characteristics:

- Like to control the environment they are in.
- Expresses humor as a practical joker.
- Originated the phrase, "No pain, no gain." Physically strong, used to hard work.
- Often suspicious due to repressed jealousy.
- Good common sense, very logical.
- Never shirks duties or responsibilities.
- Likes older, mature companions.
- Faces reality "square" in the face.
- Very punctual.
- Likes to take time to do the right thing and hates to waste time doing something over.
- Often overlooked on the job.
- Seeks high goals for themselves.
- Honestly earns their own success.
- Great concentration; loves to play chess, build jigsaw puzzles and solve a

maze or tavern puzzle.
- FOURS are so into the fine lines, at times they can miss the big picture.
- Likes the day, can work better under the sun.

FOURS seek employment in the construction professions; carpenters, masons, electricians, plumbers. They like to work with the earth as well; farming, real estate, landscaping. With the FOUR's scientific mind; research, biology and technology may appeal to them. A FOUR loves detail work; printing, mechanical or engineering may capture their fancy. Assembly work would allow them to turn raw materials in to form. FOURS could be economists, since they can evaluate worth and appraise value. These traits are also valued in banking, investing and insurance. Liking routine as they do, FOURS may find comfort in office work, shop keeping or as a computer analyst. The FOUR is very patriotic. They would make a great politician or military commander, for what is a strong government without a strong foundation.

You can expect to find the young FOUR building sandcastles or mud pies. They will also be the first in their class to get a paper route or collect cans to recycle for cash. FOURS learn at an early age in order to get ahead you have to work for it. They learn on the job rather than with a formal education. The FOUR may have been raised in a poor family or by hardworking parents developing a strong sense of responsibility and earnest.

When told to do something, the FOUR's obstinate manner can come across as crude, bossy, hateful, brutal and destructive. When they loose their originality and imagination they become boring, slow-witted, dull, melancholy, moody and lazy. FOURS can become non-conformists, refusing to honor the social norm or account for themselves.

The FOUR has to learn to lighten up on life, not to see the world only under a magnifying glass. They must bring some humor in to their life. FOURS need to make friends with THREES for this insight. FOURS also have to relax, cut loose, learn to be free without losing security. They can't block themselves in with the four restricting walls. The FIVE knows the story on that and teaches the FOUR all about freedom. When this is accomplished, the FOUR can build success and live in harmony with the limitations they have constructed for themselves.

FOURS are builders. We all need to build in order to grow. We all need to work to fully enjoy the time we get to play. FOURS will always be there to provide a home base.

Lifepath 4 Friends

Famous Lifepath 4 People

Woody Allen
Oprah
Nadia Comaneci
Brad Pitt
Babe Ruth
Mark Twain
John Hancock
Regis Philbin
Matisse
Pamela Anderson
Dalai Lama
M.C. Escher
Sigmund Freud
Donald Trump
Dolly Parton
Quentin Tarantino
Paul McCartney
Elton John
Doris Day
Michael Crichton
Thomas Jefferson
Robert Frost
Garrison Keillor
Margaret Thatcher
Uma Thurman
P.T. Barnum
Willie Nelson

Lifepath 5
I am Free

Daring, eager, active, inquisitive, this footloose adventurer needs to be free to explore the world around them. However, they don't only travel physically, but mentally and spiritually as well. Not only do they desire change, they make change. Never expect the FIVE to have only one career, one address or one love.

The name of the game is variety and they take all that is offered. They know a lot of unusual people, from unusual places, doing unusual things. Rich or poor, black or white, gay or straight, atheists or born agains, intellectuals or the off beats, the FIVE wants to know what makes them tick. And FIVES are very accepting of all types.

Loving a challenge and unafraid of taking risks, these inventive creators are full of curiosity. Their actions are induced by reason rather than emotion. However, they hate being stuck in a rut, in a routine or just plain monotony. Imagine if you will, sitting at an intersection in your car. You have to decide to go left, right or straight ahead…the FIVE wants to go UP.

FIVES are right in the middle of the pack. The four easy lessons are to one side and the four difficult lessons to the other side. It is like the Wednesday of the work week, it is a break between grammar school and high school, time to relax and have some fun, take a vacation. Being in the middle also allows the FIVE to see both sides equally, making a great go-between or arbitrator to aid in reaching decisions and conclusions. The middle also allows them to discard the past and look forward to the future.

Friends and family are always excited to hear of the FIVE'S latest escapade and at the same time worry they may never find the happiness they are apparently searching for, never realizing the happiness is in the search itself. However, the FIVE needs to be aware of the "grass is always greener" syndrome. Is the FIVE moving on due to boredom or loss of passion? Or is it for the right reason, adventure and freedom. A wise Indian chief once talked about the wolves that are constantly conflicting with each other in his brain. One is nasty, angry and always snapping. The other is sweet, playful and gentle. His grandson asked which one wins most often. The old chief's reply, "The one I feed." FIVES need to feed the positive side of freedom. If a FIVE is bored he must embrace the boredom, accept it, live with it, replace the passion. A positive FIVE moves and changes only for adventure, never to get out of a rut. The rut will only win and move with them.

Other characteristics:

- Not shy, speaks their mind.
- Lots of nervous energy (foot tapping, knuckle cracking or nail biting)
- Enthusiasm increases with interest and dies with uselessness.
- Quests knowledge from newspapers, magazines or the internet. Desires facts and draws own conclusions on current happenings.
- Avoids hard labor, prefers to make money by using their mind.
- Avid reader of the atlas, dreams of far-away places.
- Rebounds quickly, nothing keeps them down or upsets them for very long.
- Attracts the opposite sex with irresistable magnetism.
- A born gambler, but not necessarily lucky.
- Not materialistic at all. They like to change too frequently.
- Loves dinner buffets so they can eat as many different kinds of food as they want.
- Likes both day and night, sees the challenge of both.

A traveling salesman, a travel writer, a travel consultant or photojournalist will all offer the FIVE an option to promote and create while touring the countryside. A booking agent, bartender or food server, taxicab driver, explorer, investigator, test pilot, truck driver, circus performer, blackjack dealer or a homeless person will offer the FIVE the connections with unusual people and a variety of experiences necessary to hold their interest, for a little while anyway. Psychologist, inventor, detective or chemist would intrigue them as well as give them insight as to who and what ticks. A FIVE can be or do whatever he wants to and will.

Life is never dull with a FIVE; they will make their life and their mate's life exciting. And as long as they are not restricted or confined and they are allowed personal independence they will be contend in any adventuresome relationship. Fives are not domesticated or interested in heavy responsibility. If a FIVE is accepted for who they are, they can maintain a life long marriage. However, if a FIVE is not, chances are the marriage will end in a divorce. These traits of a FIVE are unbending. In a sexual relationship, a FIVE is ready, willing and able to try it all, making it interesting for both parties. FIVES have strong sexual appetites, any time is the right time, and any place is the right place.

The FIVE learns early from experiencing. They have to touch the burner to see if it is really hot. Curiosity prevails early and restraints of any kind are not recommended. FIVES will often encourage peers to break the rules with them and then use charm to escape trouble. They usually choose not to go to college, believing a degree will only limit them to one career.

FIVES deal with the five senses. They have to see, hear, touch, taste and smell everything. In contrast they may indulge on the senses, develop addictions to drugs, sex, food and/or alcohol. Beware of outbursts of temper, when the attention level is short, so is the fuse. FIVES are impatient with people who respond and move slowly. FIVES can be insincere, untruthful, and selfish and may become bored easily. They may spend more money than they have, trusting their ability to make more later.

Success is achieved when the FIVE learns how to use their freedom in a constructive manner. To do this they must look both ways. Turn back to the FOUR for a strong foundation, to understand how far you can go in each level of expression (mental, emotional, intuitive, physical). And then look to the SIX for responsibility. They must realize their potential and use the gift of freedom to go onward and upward only while developing the powers within. When progress is made on a mental level the FIVE becomes a sage.

Lifepath 5 Friends

Famous Lifepath 5 People

Charles Darwin
Abraham Lincoln
Francis Ford Coppola
Charles Barkley
Johnny Carson
Dale Earnhardt, Jr.
Benjamin Franklin
Tony Hawk
Sidney Poitier

Ellen DeGeneres
Ava Gardner
Jay Leno
Sean Penn
Steve Martin
John Steinbeck
Jane Goodall
Helen Keller
Georgia O'Keeffe

Walter Cronkite
Steven Spielberg
Louis Armstrong
Erma Bombeck
William Faulkner
Bertrand Russell
Paul Harvey
Isaac Newton
Pete Rose

Lifepath 6
I am Responsible

Softhearted, virtuous, compromising and thoughtful, this family oriented person is the epitome of love. With a strong desire to harmonize and balance through truth and justice, SIXES base all their ulterior motives on giving and receiving the love of their family and friends.

In six days all of creation was manifested according to the book of Genesis. Our higher source was able to provide a secure, loving home for all of us in a beautiful, harmonious environment. The SIX person continues on this path. You can draw a house with six lines. The SIX will make that house a home.

The SIX is compassionate, understanding, devoted and a loyal mate; a comforting, supportive, nurturing and protective parent; and a charitable, responsible, dependable and ethical community leader.

SIXES are just plain happy to be useful. They "go out of their way" in most people's eyes (especially those individuals who are odd numbers) to bring harmony to the lives of those they love. But to them it is only natural, it is not out of their way, it is simply their way.

The vibration is peace loving. The SIX believes arguing is distasteful; it is a scratch on a classical LP. In fact, the SIX rarely even criticizes anyone. They serve their town well; as a church leader, youth group counselor, civic club officer, Little League coach or delivering Meals on Wheels. They teach the people in their immediate circle to love and honor themselves and each other by setting a good example in demonstrating the meaning of love themselves.

The SIX's home is their castle. A welcome mat lies at the front door and the back one. The home is warm and cozy. Their residence makes you feel as comfortable as they do. Did I mention how well kept their home is – inside and out? SIXES will work hard to insure their family is safe, comfortable and has everything required in the home and in the heart. They are very traditional, birthdays are very special occasions, turkey is always served at Thanksgiving, ham at Easter and the star is always put on the top of the tree last on Christmas Eve, when the tree is decorated every year. SIXES expect their mates to work hard and love tradition for even more security. Remember they are not selfishly motivated; their wants are for the good of all concerned. Their family comes first. SIXES enjoy leisure time with their marriage partners to that of their friends. Often this time is spent improving the home.

Due to the SIX's idealistic view of the unity of the family, they may be involved in more than one marriage or live very harmoniously in one life long partnership. Their ties may be so strong to the family they were born in to, they may wait an extended period of time to seek out their own individual family. True love for them may come late in life.

The base for all this love comes from an innate artistic talent. The SIX has an ear for music, an eye for art and appreciation for good craftsmanship. Beauty and harmony go hand in hand. Their hobbies may involve music and/or art.

Other characteristics:

- Needs to feel needed.
- Connoisseur of fine wines and food.
- Always complimentary and truly means it.
- Smothers pets with affection, makes them a part of the happy family.
- Grows wiser everyday.
- Knows what is best for others.
- Travels for vacation purposes; always glad to come home.
- Decision-making is greatly influenced by emotions.
- Not competitive; for if they win someone else has to lose.
- If a male, could very easily become "Mr. Mom".
- Rarely ever negative.
- Dealing with money dishonestly will be a SIX's downfall.
- Early bloomer, matures quickly to take on responsibility.
- Best during the day, likes to witness the beauty.

In their desire to assist others, rather than excel self, the SIX will often become a teacher, public speaker, nurse, minister or housekeeper. Lawyers, peace officers, union leaders all believe in truth and justice. They can administer their accommodating abilities in the hotel/restaurant professions, as a chef, server, or front desk clerk. They can use their sense of color as an interior decorator, hairdresser, writer, make-up artist or in flower arranging. Even though they are physically strong and can do hard labor, the SIX prefers to use their intellect. They have a strong interest in nature making zoology, landscaping, camp counseling and farming appealing careers. SIXES often gain wealth by marrying in to it or from a family inheritance.

The SIX children often care for other younger siblings while growing up. Sometimes they may even counsel adults. They keep their room clean and orderly, while eagerly helping in other household chores. They will keep their first car spotless. The SIX matures early, becoming little "know it alls". If this life lesson was intended to be a difficult one, they may have been born in to a troubled family, with dissension and disharmony, possibly divorce. If they were sheltered as a child, the SIX may have strong convictions and religious principles appearing as an adult.

On the negative side, this SIX is meddlesome, gossipy, self-righteous, cynical, arrogant, trivial, critical and jealous. They become complacent, selfish, and too smug if they are made to feel like a doormat. Sometimes they feel too responsible, like they bit off more than they can chew.

If the SIX senses a lack of appreciation they may feel closed in and choose to move on. They must understand the constructiveness of this freedom from the FIVE. They must also learn to be judgmental, learn to analysis the situation and give only to those deserving of their love. All this can be seen in the wisdom of the SEVEN. Success in knowing how to provide, share and guide others in to a stronger and wiser independence. The result is their preservation of the values of the culture.

Lifepath 6 Friends

Famous Lifepath 6 People

Queen Elizabeth ll
Howard Hughes
Fred Astaire
James Cagney
Albert Einstein
Jesse Jackson
George W. Bush
Charles Schulz
Christopher Reeve
Joe DiMaggio
Hank Aaron
Barry Bonds
Lewis Carroll
Ralph Waldo Emerson
William Shakespeare
John Lennon
Sandra Day O'Conner
Francis Scott Key
Agatha Christie
Ben Affleck
Ray Bradbury
Thomas Edison
Stephen King
B.B. King
Mary Tyler Moore
Al Pacino
Michael Jackson

Lifepath 7
I am Spiritual

Probing, secretive, selective, and mystical; these inspirational investigators are seeking the understanding of the connection of the mind and the body. They will never take any information, be it thought, action or result at its face value. By developing the use of their mind they will capture the ultimate faith; faith in one's self.

During their formative years, up to the age fifty-four, the SEVEN learns at first by observing. In doing so, they gather enough information to ask intelligent questions. Then they are silent again, contemplating their observations and answers. When a conclusion is reached, they use their knowledge to better themselves. At the point of extreme self-confidence they will share their expertise under inquiry only. "When E.F. Hutton speaks…". These actions are not typical of the average human and hence, the SEVEN is often considered " a bit strange", traveling on a different wavelength.

Then in their wisdom years, fifty-five and on, depending on the development of the SEVEN's mind, they will either become a cynical recluse or a wily eccentric, confining themselves to live life alone and continuing to seek for all the answers. Or, full of pride and dignity, they will become the intellectual expert, a refined gentleman, connoisseur of art and literature, and an educator of us all.

SEVEN is considered a sacred number by almost all cultures. Our higher source created all this in six days and on the seventh he rested, meditated, prayed and contemplated its meaning. There are SEVEN Wonders of the World, SEVEN colors of the rainbow, SEVEN notes on a scale, SEVEN creeds and races, SEVEN steps to Heaven, SEVEN branches on the tree of life and SEVEN charkas. Flowers that have not been cross-pollinated have SEVEN petals, such as the Lotus, the emblem of Buddha's creative spirit. And I'm sure if you put your mind to it, you can come up with a few more series of SEVEN. It is thought by many that people born with a SEVEN Lifepath were alive during the life of Jesus and when they are silent their subconscious mind is taking them back to remember the experience in order to gain insight during this lifetime.

SEVEN is also considered a lucky number. And it is. But not necessarily to a person born on its path. Whenever a non-seven follows a hunch, uses their intuition and wins, it is an unexpected surprise that results in a gain, giving approval to their inner force. But a SEVEN should never gamble. To use their innate intuition, trusting it to outside forces and influence is very dangerous. It creates blind faith for the SEVEN.

The SEVEN has great trust in self; they continue to rely on soul-force. Their self-esteem comes from the confidence of their own ideas and knowledge rather then the feedback from a loving relationship. They depend on themselves for their emotional needs, rarely seeking the opinion or advice of another, especially on a personal level. They have only a few selected friends. After the SEVEN is introduced to you they will wait to listen to what you have to offer, basing their opinion of you on your opinions in general. If they find a common interest in which you may add to their knowledge, you will become their friend and you can expect them to expose their insight and charm to you. They are loyal, thoughtful, inspiring companions who will also keep your secrets.

The SEVEN gathers all the facts, inspects them together and apart, decides how they relate, fits it into a situation and comes to a conclusion they are not only satisfied with, but can put all their faith in. This ability gives them power and control. In order to accomplish all this they take the liberty to ask all the questions they want, hate evasive answers and yet do not like questions asked of them. SEVENS may even respond to a personal question in a fit of rage if the answer would unmask them or expose a flaw in their intelligence level. The phenomenal intrigues them. In their quest for knowledge the unexplained provides them with a deeper understanding of life. SEVENS link the known with the unknown. They will constantly weigh the facts of science and religion. Many a SEVEN has found enlightenment in the metaphysical world, where a balance of compassion and insights sparks their interests.

SEVENS worry a lot; the imagination works overtime, allowing the situation to appear far worse than it really is.

A SEVEN requires a lot of rest, peace and quiet. Especially if they are both physically and mentally active. Meditation offers a return to serenity. As does a connection to nature. They must leave the crowded city to seek their inner self on the shores of the seas and the tops of the mountains.

A SEVEN enjoys and appreciates art. They see the beauty of the piece, then looks at the individual brush strokes, each stitch, every note of the composition to better understand the craftsmanship.

Other characteristics:

- Must learn to be alone without being isolated.
- Dislikes imitations or copycats.
- Skilled with their hands.
- Likes certain foods, cooked a certain way.
- Possesses ESP.
- Sometimes they talk to themselves.
- Searches for and enjoys the quintessence.
- During a discussion with a SEVEN, you may get the last word if you take it; but during a disagreement they always get the last word.
- Enjoys stringed instruments.
- Loves nature and wild animals.
- Enjoys comfortable clothes made of soft fabrics; easy to "think" in.
- Hates noise pollution.
- Strong desire for perfection in self and everything else – human or material.
- Start most conversations with, "Can you tell me why…?"
- Loves to travel to faraway lands; having the opportunity to study different cultures first hand.
- Displays their humor in dry wit, allowing them to ridicule the less intelligent while displaying his own.
- Not swayed by sentiment; dislikes any display of uncontrolled emotion.
- You can't change them; they have to want to change in order for a change to happen.
- Lives in a comfortable home for self, not meant to be shared with others.
- Sees no real value in money, it is only printed-paper, which cannot be backed by the government. Doesn't see security in the dollar, so they spend all they get, living beyond their means. Heaven help them with a credit card.
- Best at night. They form the questions during the day and think of the answers in the quiet, still darkness of the night. Answers also come to them in dreams.

To begin with, the SEVEN will never wear a uniform, so that eliminates a lot of careers already. More interested in concepts rather than products, you are bound to find the SEVEN in investigation and spiritual fields. Religious researchers, CIA agents, cultural experts, engineers, inventors and priests will most likely be SEVENS. With their efficiency in math and science you will find astrology, homeopathic medicine, numerology, psychic healing, navigating and technical work to their liking. Their love of art would open the doors as a curator. Of course analytically speaking, psychiatrists, librarians and economists may walk this path. Magicians are often SEVENS. Whatever field they pick, they are guaranteed to be the expert in that field.

As a child, the SEVEN is quiet and sneaky. They are always just around the corner listening and never let you in on what they are up to. They communicate in questions; their questions. They prefer to do all the asking, especially regarding disciplinary actions. They require more privacy than other children. Their parents should encourage sports and other outside interests during their high school years in order to bring them "out" early in life. They should always be shown both sides of any situation. Life can start out being difficult if one delay after another holds them back. Progress should be quick in the early years. They will respond to approval and appreciation.

A negative SEVEN has no depth, they are fault finding, deceitful, intimidating and sarcastic. They often find enjoyment in talking over people's heads. They may use their mind to trick and to scheme. Too formal and unemotional, they may appear lazy and depressive. The SEVEN may even choose to drink or steal in prevention of facing reality. No answers spiritually will leave the SEVEN an agnostic.

In order to balance their lives, the SEVEN must learn compassion by developing a warm heart and realize the domestic responsibilities of the SIX; and the balance of the power and value of the dollar from the EIGHT. If they can enjoy the good company and material pleasures of life, they will achieve the ultimate in wisdom and faith.

Lifepath 7 Friends

Famous Lifepath 7 People

Princess Diana	Johnny Depp	Jackie Robinson
John F. Kennedy	Aleister Crowley	Katharine Hepburn
Ansel Adams	Muhammad Ali	Charles Atlas
Marilyn Monroe	George W. Bush	Dr. Phil
Johnny Cash	Jim Henson	Andy Warhol
Jerry Garcia	Louis L'Amour	Jimmy Stewart
Danielle Steel	Woody Guthrie	Tommy Hilfiger
Louis Pasteur	Jesse James	Eric Clapton
Mister Rogers	Sylvia Plath	Barbara Streisand

Lifepath 8
I am Powerful

Dynamic, high-powered, zealous, masterful; these highly respected financiers are on a path to achieve success on the business level by combining their ambition and integrity. Their ultimate goal is not just the money, they love authority and power.

Pushing themselves to succeed, the EIGHT overcomes obstacles with ease. They drive themselves hard, working long hours. They have extremely good judgment where people's characters are concerned. The EIGHT can size them up upon the moment they first meet them. It is at this time they decide if they would both be a good worker for them and be able to get the required job done proficiently and on time, or if they would be someone for whom they could work, a person they could respect and take orders from. Either way, the outcome must promote and add growth to the EIGHT.

The figure EIGHT is an upright sign of infinity, which is a spiral motion joining two circles. Infinity is the state of being endless; unlimited extent of time and space; absolute perfection. Metaphysically it means " What goes around, comes around" or "As above, so below". But, where does it start? Where does it end? It is the only number that has no starting point, or ending point, it just goes on and on. It can also be written forward and backward with ease. Therefore complete reversals are possible. Hense, the vibration represents the building of huge empires or great fortunes lost. It controls the ebb and the flow. Circumcisions used to be performed on the eighth day of the baby boy's life.

The EIGHT takes on a leadership role quite naturally. They are not bold or pushy, but rather reserved and shy on the outside, while on the inside they have a strong intense drive to take and remain in control. They don't beat around the bush, but are very direct in their explanation of needs to be done. Always very busy working, EIGHTS like to see everyone busy working. They know everyone's potential and encourages others to succeed. When they critic, they are always fair about it. They will not allow personality conflicts to interfer with getting the job done. Afraid to take risks and an innate need for security keeps the EIGHT from becoming self-employed.

EIGHTS are professional problem-solvers and troubleshooters. Their intuition allows them to see the whole situation, recognize the weakness of the plan, and delegate tasks to the right employees to get the job done, gain control and allow the situation to run smoothly; just like the figure eight. EIGHTS are masterminds.

Even though the EIGHT attracts money easily, it is not a lucky number. EIGHTS realize they have to work for their money, not that hard mind you, but they are better off not gambling. They are practical and down to earth. They do not fantasize of winning the state lottery, nor have they dreams or visions of grandeur. EIGHTS see things realistically. That's good, because they could get caught up in the thrill and lose it all.

Loyal and devoted mate, the EIGHT has a difficult time expressing feelings. To them it is a sign of weakness. They do love deeply and feel as though their ability to bring pride to the family name shows more love than a tender touch or a sweet nothing whispered in the ear of their mate. They want their children to be proud of who they are, because of who the EIGHT is. They may find it hard to show affection, but have no difficulty expressing emotions. They like to quarrel, usually shouting off about repeated mistakes, fear of fidelity, or lack of effort in carrying their share of the load. An EIGHT really likes being married; unattached, they are lonely.

With their great physical strength, stamina and endurance, the EIGHT is a proven sports figure. Many of the same qualities are used in both business and sports. They have strong concentration powers, see other team's weaknesses, take control, make decisions, love to compete and lead the team to victory.

To play the part, the EIGHT has to look the part. They dress fastidiously, drive an expensive, well made automobile, joins the country club of the elite, owns the state of the art electronics and belongs to the health club of the in crowd. To be important and successful the EIGHT starts with appearances.

Dramatic ordeals are always part of the EIGHT's path, they are victims of tragedy. They love control and when they feel they have none, they unknowingly create trauma. They become ill or have an accident. The EIGHT provides a good excuse for their weakness, plus it attracts attention and pampering which they love but do not like to admit to it. As they mature and have learned better how to use their natural talents, they will lighten up, calm down, and start going with the natural flow of the EIGHT. Many on this path actually look younger at forty than they did at twenty. EIGHTS are like Pisceans, they live to a ripe old age.

Other characteristics:

- Likes to know what's going on in the world.
- Understands human nature.
- Bored by routine, they like upsets so they can use their talents to mend all.
- Have many interests.
- Compares their status to that of their friends.
- Sees only black or white, never grey.
- Attracted to older mates.
- Works for truth and justice.
- College degree is not necessary; believes in business you either have it or you don't. Good business sense cannot be taught.
- A venturesome Wheeler Dealer.
- Shows signs of being chauvinistic.
- A good friend, or bitter enemy.
- Subtle sense of humor.
- No such thing as a procrastinating EIGHT.
- Likes both the day and night; they can be powerful anytime.

Corporation, industry and government administration employment is right up number EIGHT's ladder. The larger the company, the more people they get to pass on their way to the top. Also they have the potential of having power over a greater number of people. They are here to use their mental abilities, not physical abilities. The EIGHT is also attracted to the political arena, the campaigning would be challenging and the result would provide power. As a banker, stockbroker, realtor or antique dealer they could control, value and deal with the money. The literary field; printing, publishing, magazines, newspapers, dealing in current events would hold the EIGHT's interest. The drama of acting, boxing or archaeology would excite them. As a bandleader they could orchestrate. Whatever the EIGHT chooses, it will offer lots of security and have great room for advancement. Regardless of the livelihood, the EIGHT will definitely master it.

Don't expect the EIGHT tikes to take an afternoon nap. You might refer to the young EIGHT as "straight arrows" as they are growing up. As kids, they maintain good grades, involve themselves in sports, may even be class president and have a part time afternoon and weekend job. If a female, chances are the parents were hoping for a boy and so she spends a great deal of effort proving her masculine side. Or maybe the parents were very authoritive, intelligent, religious or ethnic, in which case, the EIGHT has had to struggle for direction. As teenagers, they may have had an incompetent employer, leaving them with the urge to do better at that job when they grew up.

If unscrupulous, greedy, fatalistic or ruthless, the EIGHT is not able to balance themselves. They may abuse their power, be domineering, impatient of others, oppressive, intense, even blunt in their actions on their off days. They may receive no pleasure in achievement if status is not apparent, success is not always felt through income. EIGHTS are sometimes revengeful and power hungry. They may prove to be selfish with material goods, or be jealous of someone else's.

EIGHTS require a natural rhythm to keep the flow of the eight going. They must gain self-confidence and learn to relax from the SEVEN vibrations. And then look to the NINE for love and a softer nature. They must deal more patiently with others. When they can give and take as the figure EIGHT, the infinite and finite will groove in harmony.

Lifepath 8 Friends

Famous Lifepath 8 People

Bette Davis	Martin Scorsese	Liz Taylor
Joan Collins	Yasser Arafat	Neil Armstrong
Lucille Ball	Alexander Graham Bell	Bill Clinton
Bob Dylan	Mary Baker Eddy	John Paul ll
Nelson Mandela	Wayne Gretzky	Mickey Mantle
George Patton, Jr.	Diane Keaton	Derek Jeter
Renee Zellweger	Picasso	Condoleezza Rice
Michelangelo	Paul Newman	Nostradamus
George Orwell	Martha Stewart	Dennis Rodman

Lifepath 9
I am Compassionate

Charismatic, patient, bold, magnetic and independent, this universal metaphysician is here to teach and to heal mankind. Their path is to establish a balance of the body, mind and soul on what may very well be their last incarnation. NINES have very ambitious intentions and the highest ideals of life.

In the numerology world, NINES are referred to as "old souls", such as the astrology world views Pisceans. NINES have had many previous lives, taken all the paths one through eight, possibly even the NINE lifepath prior to this life. They can see themselves in all of mankind. This is obvious by the magic of the number NINE. If you multiply nine by any of the other numbers, the addition of the two-digit total will always be nine. 3x9=27(2+7=9), 7x9=63(6+3=9) And if you add nine to any of the other numbers it will not change the vibration of that number. 2+9=11(1+1=2) 6+9=15(1+5=6) Get the picture? NINES have the ability to relate to each and every one of the other eight lifepaths, they can see all the "other sides" so to speak. They can see the good in every single person. NINES have learned not to be prejudice, for they have "walked in everyone's shoes".

NINE is a number of beginnings and endings. It takes nine months to create a miracle, the miracle of birth. That is 270 days (2+7+0=9) to produce a new physical body for a spirit to inhabit. In the book of Revelations, the number "666" is made in reference to the "number of the beast". 6+6+6=18 and 1+8=9 "666" is the number of the outcome of the union of the physical and the spiritual. Will this soul be lost or saved? The answer lies in the path of the NINE. Having experienced all of the paths of life, they must decide to be good or evil, a God or the Devil. In John, it is written that Christ, on the ninth hour nailed to the cross said, "It is finished".

As a NINE they are very idealistic. They believe in a perfect world or at least their ability to heal its wounds. During their early years, they were on the roller coaster of life. They would go to extremes in moods and in luck, from living in a utopia to the deepest of depressions. NINES' reaction to outside circumstances vacillated between high and low. They excite themselves with new ideas, new products, and new friends and then when they see their imperfections it brings them down, way down. As they mature they control their ideals of material items and soon after that they learn to accept people for who they are. However, most people will bore NINES. They do hold on to their expectations of themselves. And at this point they learn to look within, realizing all experiences are neutral and their reaction makes it good or bad. NINES become understanding, kind, tolerant, generous and cooperative with others. They find inner strength, energy and love. NINES will also receive wisdom from the universe, becoming spiritual and broad-minded. Finally in control of their life, NINES are able to show others the way, giving them control of life itself. NINE is the closest number to God.

As they attempt to gain control, still fluctuating between ecstasy and depression, NINES' life is traumatized by accidents, rather than disease or illness. People who choose not to gain control at all will get dis-eased. Accidents are more likely to happen to those who are on a path and either loses balance and trip or fall so to speak. They pick themselves up, brush off and continue down the road. That is a NINE. When they come to realize that this life is only a small part of the whole universe, they are able to let go. Relieving the tension, they won't fall as often. And if they become too attached to the material world; cherishing items and hoarding money, fate has a way of stepping in and removing it all in a very dramatic way; death of a business partner, divorce, fire, or earthquake. The NINE is then forced to release that which anchors them to the physical world. This is a spiritual path. The NINE who travels light, travels fast. The typical NINE will recover quickly and rise again. It is almost as if the NINE has to prove to themselves on this path that they have mastered all the lessons of life, so they are challenged by all the numbers during this one short lifetime.

NINES are attracted to other energetic, self-confident, dynamic and spiritual people. They are the marrying type, hoping to complete their life with the union of another enlightened soul. This is usually an older; more cultured individual rather than a younger, needier type. Even though they love deeply with much affection and compassion, their mate must understand this romantic lover will not limit them self to one person or one family. NINES truly do love mankind and generate their love by going to great lengths to share their insight on life to all their brothers and sisters of the world. If NINES attach them self to one person they are not fulfilling their mission. And if one tries to restrict a NINE in a marriage, that marriage will end abruptly in a divorce.

Self-motivated, empathetic and ultra-talented, NINES are super sensitive. They see the world with great feeling, responding not only to the environment and the people, but to sound, color, smell and touch. NINES cry easily, get goose bumps when aroused and a chill up the spine with a fright in the night. Their artistic talents and imagination can run wild by all of this. NINES creativity must find an outlet for this expression.

Other characteristics:

- Gains success through disaster.
- Loves to serve humanity.
- Seeks perfection. Likes the best: attracts the best.
- Deals in broad concepts.
- NINES have luck; it is totally different than being lucky.
- Quick-thinking individuals.
- Easy come; easy go.
- Travels a lot, close and abroad. They like to learn how others live and love.
- Uses intuition wisely.
- Hates pettiness.
- Innate ability to communicate with animals; domesticated and wild.
- Habits are hard to break. Should avoid smoking, drinking and drugs.
- Has a Heart of Gold.
- Chooses their own lifestyle.
- Has a talent for knowing something about another human being and bringing it to their attention in amazement.
- Often falls in love with love. And then is hurt by reality. As a young adult will experience many short time relationships.
- Must learn to cherish the beauty of a lasting friendship.
- Best at night for it is harder to see the imperfections in the dark.

Career oriented, NINES direct their leadership qualities toward education or politics and their healing qualities toward medicine or priesthood. NINES hold a strong urge to "do for others". NINES can do and be anything, remember they have walked in all types of shoes, boots, sandals, sneakers or even barefoot. Serving many, not just a few will prove NINES' success.

As a youth, they may have been the rescuer, climbing a tree to save a cat or saving another's life from drowning. They were the father when playing house and the surgeon when playing doctor. NINES often mimic foolishness of their peers and elders. They are precocious and understand fully the feeling of a disciplinary action by a parent. NINES matured early in life, maybe missing out on the carefree attitude of adolescence. They may have good intentions or be extra critical and overact emotionally during the formative years. A hard life lesson would place him in a family with aloof parents, with a devil may care air about them. This would be very difficult for the NINE child.

Not wanting to limit their potential or face everyday realities, an out of balance NINE will become aimless, selfish, heartless and cynical. All the benefits of the previous lessons can also reappear as negatives. Dissatisfied with less than a perfect world, NINES could be challenged by possessiveness, confusion, indecision, prejudice, stubbornness and vulgarity.

NINES must look both ways to balance this lesson. To the EIGHT they see the importance of a natural flow. NINES must learn to give out true love, knowledge and reward without expecting its return. But, much to their delight it will flow back, even stronger. On the other side is the TEN, or God, represented by the strong, straight stroke of the one and all encompassing circle of the divine power. Wait, isn't that what produces the figure NINE as well? A circle and a straight line. Let go and let God. It is said one is truly enlightened when one sees God in everything.

Lifepath 9 Friends

Famous Lifepath 9 People

Dustin Hoffman	Henry Fonda	Lance Armstrong
David Letterman	Elvis	Al Capone
Jimmy Carter	Charlie Chaplin	Ray Charles
Julia Child	Cher	Alan Greenspan
Carl Jung	Morgan Freeman	Jack Nicholson
Charles Lindbergh	Anais Nin	Yoko Ono
Frank Lloyd Wright	Gilda Radner	Nikola Tesla
Hunter S. Thompson	Robin Williams	Kurt Vonnegut, Jr.
Serena Williams	Jonas Salk	Jason Lee

More

The MORE is how you can use this knowledge to create a happier and healthier life for you and everyone else whose name and number appears in this workbook. This is the part where you understand each and every Lifepath number and can now appreciate yourself and all the people that are part of your life. Everyone is interested in building self-esteem. It definitely aids in obtaining personal success, enjoying long-lasting relationships and maintaining healthy bodies. By grouping your acquaintances by their Lifepaths you should be able to recognize their likes and hence better understand the force of each path. Now you can use it to compliment, acknowledge, guide, encourage, insure and accept your friends for who they are and why they do the things they do. No longer will you question their actions or try to change them. And better yet, you will know and understand yourself as well. Soon you will be able to see good in all mankind. And when you can do that, you can help them build their individual self-esteem and aid them to create their own positive attitude.

Attitude. Our attitude toward anything at all is completely within our control. So take that control and make it a daily goal to have a positive attitude. This is made easy for us through the wonderful world of numbers and the spiritual understanding of life. It is the awareness of our creative force. It is knowing you have a soul. It is your connection with a higher source. Many people use many ways to become true believers; be it prayer, meditation or affirmations. And some of us are blocked, hurried or just find no need to believe at all. There are many other tools that help us link our physical world to our spiritual world. Numbers is just the one that cleared my mind and created my positive attitude.

As you analyze each group on their Lifepath page, keep in mind that the young and the old are better examples of each path. For as a child we are free to be ourselves and as we age we return to what we believe we are truly meant to be. As for the age in the middle, we are often confused by our peers who are trying to change us.

There are really only eight Lifepaths demonstrated by the nine individual expressions. The Lifepath Nine represents the completion or integration of all the previous eight lessons. There are some very distinct differences between the odd and the even expressions. You may even call them opposites or opposing forces.

Odd (1,3,5,7)	Even (2,4,6,8)
Interested in what it "means".	Interested in what it "is".
Loves to have fun.	Loves to work.
Independent ambitions.	Group ambitions.
Thinks of the future in wonder.	Thinks of the past for facts.
Learns by experiencing.	Learns through education.
Where am I going?	Where have I been?
Knows a little about a lot.	Knows a lot about a little.
Creative.	Informative.
Explores the new and different.	Investigates the old and reliable.
Abstract.	Practical.
Idealistic.	Mundane.
Likes individual sports.	Likes team sports.

Remember the magic of the number NINE? NINES are able to accept and understand all the Lifepaths. They would read down these lists by putting the word "and" between the opposing forces. They want to know what it means and what it is. They love to have fun and love to work. By accepting both sides equally they prove their love of self, mankind and GOD.

In my opinion, every single person is compatible to another, if the desire is present. First, compare the paths of both individuals in a relationship, recognize the likes and dislikes, the strengths and the weaknesses and accept what you find. If the paths are both "odds" or both "evens", this acceptance should be easy. And if you are talking about one of each, just look at what you can learn from this relationship. The compatibility is the reward of numerology.

Success is knowing you have a soul. Souls feel no pain. So in reality, it is good health that is the reward. Knowing, understanding and accepting the differences of man will bring contentment and happiness to your life. No one ever dies of a disease if he has a happy heart and deems himself successful.

Now if I may, I would like to end this workbook of the numbers with a poem my father sent to me a few years ago.

I cannot ask you to smile all my smiles, cry all my tears,
share all my hopes, dream all my dreams.
For you have your own smiles, tears, hopes and dreams,
which are yours alone.
But if you wish to walk with me awhile, I will smile with your laughter,
hurt in your tears, hope for your hopes, and listen to your dreams.

CPSIA information can be obtained at www.ICGtesting.com
Printed in the USA
LVOW09s0513171113

361617LV00004B/24/A